# Poems and Versions

Also by David Wright from Carcanet
*Selected Poems*

# POEMS AND VERSIONS

# David Wright

CARCANET

First published in 1992 by
Carcanet Press Limited
208-212 Corn Exchange Buildings
Manchester M4 3BQ

A CIP catalogue record for this book
is available from the British Library
ISBN 0 85635 963 7

The publisher acknowledges financial assistance
from the Arts Council of Great Britain

Set in 10pt Palatino by Bryan Williamson, Darwen
Printed and bound in England by SRP Ltd, Exeter

*To Oonagh*

Lyke the Audience, so uttir thy language.

# Contents

## Encounter in a Glass

Skin coarse, bird-shotted nose, the flesh loose,
Almost a hammock underneath the chin;
Eyebrows en brosse – a zareba, that one –
A sprout of hair in earhole and nostril,
Lines traversing like mountain trods the forehead –
I almost wondered who the fellow was.

I knew him well enough, the non-stranger,
Yet was – as, despite a remembered face,
One can't identify some familiar
Acquaintance in an unaccustomed place –
About to make the oddest of faux pas:
To offer him my seat, and call him sir.

## On a Fiftieth Birthday

Balanced in water, between bones, head down,
Diver into light and air, I waited,
Living on the heartbeating and breath of
My then world, to plunge into that other.

Fifty years I have pumped my own blood, and
Found my sustenance in a larger room.
Constellations wheel about me; under
The two legs I balance on, solid ground.

I did not ask for these endowments, or
Being. An envelope of air sustains
My breath and what I feed on. What body
Of laws, matter, living birds, fish, flesh and

Vegetable, has so nourished and hemmed
Me like that other I escaped from? Time
Passes and is a strange condition.
Like you, like him or her, I chanced my arm,

Or had it chanced for me, by outbreaking
Into circumstance prepared, haphazard,
A net of choice and a fork of causes.
Half a century! Thanks for the present.

## Juxtapositions

Six decades gone and one to come,
In summer leaves I read, autumn.

July foliage, winter form:
Beech in leaf and barebones elm.

I saw a salmon leap and fail,
Fail and leap where water fell.

A wake of wild geese flying by
A river mirroring their sky.

Low river, slow river, heron
Slow also, loth to go, going.

## Lustra

Seven lustra, seven selves,
First and blessed is the child's.
Five senses and a Ma and Pa;
To wander in, an Africa;
And music – organ, violin,
All voices – animal, human;
Then ear is dead and eye is all.

Pitied, unpitying, the boy
With the energy of all young
Resilient to enjoy
What is withheld as it were given,
Finds that he has an eye to listen,
To foliage uttering the wind,
To language, music in his mind:

Words are notes that he can hear.
Next, half a boy and half a man
With penis ripe and pubic hair,
Blackheads and doubt to torment him,
He finds his world no longer fair:
But could he feel as he felt then!
If there's a Muse, she found him when

Experience taught him what he'd read:
Art illumines, but cannot teach;
It's life that learns us; and as youth
Becomes man, discovers truth
As beautiful in the banal –
In what gets prayed for, daily bread:
The common common to us all.

Nel mezzo! No, more than half way
With nothing done, and still to learn.
The hill's been climbed, the path winds down
To the evening valley.
Now he has a companion
And raises here and there a stone
Marker for others who may come.

Descending in his prime between
His youth and age, now is the time
He knows himself, what he has been,
What he will be and cannot be,
And so reflects in action
Between two worlds, the shortening
To be, and lengthening what has been.

Looking and going back, he goes
To a natal not a native land,
At home and homeless whether he's
In Africa or England:
Divided in either case,
The prospect from his window is
A Magaliesberg or Pennine.

*　　*　　*

A change of room, a change of view:
The Eden river runs below
A bosky lime and dying elm;
An elder bush is white as snow
That winter brought so long ago,
For summer's here, and spring has been,
And there's an autumn still to come.

The grand climacteric, the change
Of life begins when those who made
The man depart, and one by one
Assume the silence of the grave
And turn, as in the tale, to stone:
Their likenesses are all we have,
They live in us, who are alone.

The tally of threescore and ten
Has been made up. Desire shall fail
Because he goes to his long home,
The dust to dust – but where, the soul
That in the living world was made
Out of delight and passion
To know, or not know, all is well?

5

## Moles

Four of them gibbeted on a barbed wire
With blindslit eyes, in slateblue overcoats,
Guerrilla captains of an insurrection.
Yes, they look sinister,
These representatives of an underground vote
Which was not cast in our favour.
Their lineaments obstinate, keeping secret
The subversion underfoot.
Wide, spadelike, callous hands, able to sap
Beneath appearance, mine and countermine.
Do not be deceived by smallness.
Heaps of spoil erupt like pimples –
What goes on in cells and galleries
Threaded below solid earth, the surface?
You never see them except dead like this.
Ears without conches; broad, short forearms;
Muzzles obtusely pointed; length, six inches;
Erect fur, dense and velvet. They are
Frequent as pigeons; leave their signature
In this place and in that, like an infection.

## Properties

Concurrent unconversable animal
Lives, habitants of this half-acre garden
To which we have title, but at best part-own!
– The robin's territory stretches from
That corner of the wood to a walled field,
Involves and overlaps our lawn and orchard.
And there are other coexistent kingdoms:
The unseen owl's; bats' flight-paths; besides which
Who can tell what the moles below lay claim to?
Co-proprietors of the same ground ignore
Each other, of their own kind only wary.
The robin gives me right of way; I him;
He none to other robins, nor I to men;
What's private to me's private too for him.

## Owl

An owl heard, but not seen; our unwild doves
Told us of him by never coming back.
It was an owl, we said, or else a hawk,
When, absent in the morning, at noon too,
Absent by evening, dead now for certain,
One of our birds, never again appearing,
Bespoke the presence of a predator.
At dusk, over the river, an owl's cry;
The beeches, cloaks of blackness; it was him.

One day last week, caught up with sunlight, the
Many birds, all tribes, blackbird in the van,
Tit, sparrow, chaffinch, collared dove, robin,
Scolding commotion, even the wren made one,
Diving high up, fluttering among foliage
There, just below the beech-tree's topmost bough,
Drew us; what was the matter? A shadow
Shadowed in hundred shadows, aloft there
Lodged, a focus of united fury.

Immobile, brown, and huge, not one to bat
An eyelid, the brown owl; he did not have to.

## White Christmas

Outside the window, snow that fell
In so large flakes two weeks ago
Recedes, reluctant as the thaw;
The bare, black water of the river
Moves slowly, hardly moves at all.

The disappointment of the year
Reflected in a sky that's clogged
With grey, a woollen sheet of cloud;
All bone and feather, the blackbird.

The longest night's about to fall
Thickening a dead gleam of snow
That upon ground too long, too long
Has lain, and burned the grass below.
On such an evening, Christ be born.

## Remembering Tennyson

Of verse and shadow, Somersby,
I think, and of a summer early
Morning under over-leafy
Elms, memorial and immense,
Lifting above lane and barton
Heavy-leaved and hidden limbs
Where flat Lincolnshire is hilly.

Lost in a thicket, a chapel;
Its graveyard grass is long and wet.
A Tudor manor with a moat
About it, next a vicarage
That hides its lawn and garden with
A Georgian nondescript façade:
Here Arthur Hallam walked and talked.

With flutterings of many leaves
And colloquy of silences
Of many days and many hours
The georgic quiet is weighted.
Too early yet for men to stir,
A soundless world of weed and briar,
Fields yellow-green and ordinary,

Enclose the hamlet – a surround
Of times long gone and here for ever.
Dust lies upon those hedgerow boughs
Unclipped in summer gaudery
As his brown brook hobbles under
Trails of bramble, travelling
To find a level and far sea.

## On the River Avon, near Stratford

He is, of course, the genius of the place,
That is, of midland England, whose flatness
Rescues it from unreasonable beauty;
A pleasant, unremarkable country
Watered by its river Avon, whose source is
The middle point of England, near Naseby.

I knew its reaches well: at least from Evesham
As far as Warwick. Then I was a boy
And it was the summer armadas came over
With the full moon, flying to Birmingham
And back again, unladen, before morning.
I saw the cattle drowsing in the fields,
And black elms ponder over scarcely pacing
Water, while white spokes of light, far off,
Walked on the horizon until All Clear.
And there my boat lay, floating on the water,
Well above Bidford; ready to go on.

The time, like all times, furious; my voyage
Frivolous, without aim, peripheral.
But now I feel its meaning, as I did then,
A realization that a golden age
Exists; at all times, though no age is golden;
And that it is enough to see it once:
A derelict park, receding pastoral,
An intense present, ever caught between
All that must be because of what has been.

## James Ward's Gordale Scar

It's not a painting but a celebration,
This canvas, which seems huger than the room
It broods in, pastoral yet sybilline:
These hanging cliffs and brown romantic shades,
Darkness composed, and solitude imaged.

As for its subject – upon the high limestone
Moors above Settle, you'll find Gordale Scar
Deflated, an authentic diminution
Of the assertion of its picture here:
The gloom is not the mood, the scale is smaller.

No reality but in imagination:
The painting is more real than the place;
More than the thing is its interpretation,
Or than its interpreter, whose bias
Of feeling, here contained, transmutes to vision.

## After Hugo von Hofmannsthal

'The depths must be concealed. Where? On the surface.'
And is that why one reveres the banal
And dramatic no-drama of actual life,
And unforeseeable let-down of the real?
Or where is there any blue, like blue of mid-
Atlantic mirroring azure air, that's less
Azure than the colour the surface reflects
Under which a weight, a silence of fathoms,
Like the blood and muscle of a limb, lies hid?

## Heureux qui, comme Ulysse

Shopwindowsful of tat, flaking gimcrack collonades,
Tearoom, bazaar, bottle-store; the Sunray Herbalist
(Dried crocodile feet, skins of snakes, powdered bark and leaves)
Ousting Franks' Pharmacy. A City-Stad goes by
The blistered SLEGS VIR BLANKES. Louis Botha Avenue
Rolls unchanged between the changes – where is Graaff's? and where,
Airy and Edwardian under wooden balconies,

The Orange Grove Hotel? As I used to long ago,
Though *retourné plein d'usage*, and perhaps *raison*,
I look toward Magaliesberg, smaller on the sky
Line of the high veld, diminuendo to the eye;
Changed they are but changeless is their image in my mind.
Time forgives and colours with foliage and decay
Bald concrete and raw vistas; pacific woods have grown;

Only the same light bleaching from the angles of the day
Holds in clear, fanatic air, the contour of my home –
Whose low, long range of kopjes white bijou villas climb
Close above a tinroofed grid and traffic-sparkled plain,
Bungalows in baking gardens, glint of trolley-wires;
Mediocre, seedy, a tentacular suburb,
Childhood prospect, banal, glanced again at and beloved.

## Changes

*For Walter Andrewes*

A small walled garden with a heavy loquat,
Coarse African lawn, declining sun saying
Goodnight, your tea's gone cold. An old man under
A straw trilby, sitting, looking. Not at

His trained rose climbing slowly up a trellis
But at I don't know what – a Twenties London?
Tibbalds not Theobalds Road unbombed; Harold
Monro's bookshop in the goldbeaters' quarter

Just round the corner? My contemporaneous
Memories chase his. A veld here, and donga,
Waterhole for duiker in suburban Jo'burg
When his Devonshire Street held Georgian houses.

15

## Easter at Machadodorp
*To Patrick Cullinan*

Windpumps twinkling metal sails
And rivers embroidered with green,
A dirt road, slower horizons;
Well I remember going by
Machadodorp in '51.

Now, bar the odd oniony spire
Its limewashed church points at the sky,
Nothing that I remember's here.
A chromium and formica
Cafe selling chips and Coca-Cola

To helmeted Easter riders
Tells, more than dead grass or turned leaves,
It's later in a later year;
A new macadam ribbon bonds
Maputo to Pretoria.

When first I came, an early green
Of summer lit up thorn and tree
Where autumn with an arid hand
Now lays a browner colour on
The bareback koppies riding to

Their summit pile in Swaziland.
Forty miles from Machadodorp
I look at them from your farm stoep:
At frontier mountains looming change
Half lost beyond a high valley.

Where aboriginal bush
Crawls down a kloof which hides the stream
That feeds, below, a trout-filled dam,
Above, a buzzard from the steppes
Impends on broad and roundedged wings

As two never-bridled horses
Canter across their paddock to
Earn their keep with beauty – do
They know? or gallop out of joy?
– Such peace is merely apparent,

But being apparent, exists,
If merely for the moment. Yet
The mayfly moment's all we've got.
A hidden sawmill that devours
The pines that shield it, primes the farm:

Uneconomic – nothing pays –
Anachronous and Horatian
Pastoral; useless; an enclave
And out of touch. But I don't know.
A sort of happiness for all

Sorts with this insecure content.
The proper values spread around,
Not to count but be counted on,
Embodied here, and therefore mortal,
Touch upon what is permanent.

One day we climbed the neighbour hill
And saw, through soft cloud blowing by,
The panorama of a maze
Of predial convolute valleys
From horizon to horizon:

Wild land no longer wilderness,
Its myriad antelopes dead or gone
With the hyena and lion;
A cornucopia of species
Eliminated for our own.

Best not look back or forward here.
Those underfoot protean weeds
And grasses, lilies by the stream,
Wild dagga and composite flowers,
With the sun for good fortune

Will likely repeat, autumn by
Autumn the colours of the scene
As they did when, those years ago,
Even before the trees were grown
To yield the beams that built your home,

I saw the green of summer burn
About the spire and the town
As I passed through Machadodorp;
And your unhandled valley was
Raw and houseless, rock and grass.

## The Weaver-bird's Nest
### Homage to Guy Butler

From the corner of my window
– While, brown and troubled, floods below
Eden carrying autumnal
Colour to Corby and Carlisle –
Hangs a hanging nest, a weaver
Bird's, that hung beside Fish River
From the spiked ramage of a thorn
That other, African autumn.
It hangs, souvenir of a day
We drove to Salem and the sea
Looking for European bygones,
Our English-windowed Settler farms,
Where Bartolomeu Diaz set
Our cross in fourteen eighty eight.

Stitched with bill and skill it was,
This yellow bobble, woven grass;
Whenever I look at it,
Old friend of mine (though seldom met),
I see your river wind and twist
At its enormous distances;
Think of you, stranger to Europe,
As an autochthonous voice
Of the country, tongue, and kin
To which you and I were born;
Which I have left, while you have stayed,
Understood and interpreted
The dry parochial distances,
Adverse and inverted seasons.

While now, in Africa, it is
Your usual promise-little spring
With foreign orchards blossoming,
Gales and flattening rains begin
The overture to my autumn
To shake down yet unyellowed leaves
As, like our native weaver-bird,
I find a word to bind a word

To knit the ravel of a verse
To bear you *mes devoirs* across
Divides of time as well as sea:
For, in this kind of saying, we
Address a now that is not yet
And so forward the living moment.

## A Letter to C.H. Sisson

Dear Charles,
          I think that we first met
At Henekey's in Kingley Street,
And more than twenty years ago.
You'd not find two men more unlike –
I mean the civil servant who
Was always civil (servant to
The devil, as he defined it)
And the habitué of Soho
Who'd never had a proper job,
Like nearly everyone he knew –
George Barker, Cronin, Kavanagh,
Bacon, the Roberts, Swift and Freud,
Maclaren-Ross and John Heath-Stubbs,
Gascoyne and Sydney Graham too –
There's not much left now of that crowd.
And yet it seems we understood
Each other, if I may say so,
Before we actually met:
Your verses opened on my desk
Up in that garret in New Row
The vision, spare and authentic,
Of an intellect I now know
As savage, luminous, and just.
    But let me cavil if I may:
A matter of temperament
Perhaps; but even now I find
For all that you appreciate
The underlay of the absurd
Beneath each surface, comedy
Of things as much as *lacrimae
Rerum*, I'd say your outlook is
– Although justified by logic –
One that, to what I call my mind,
Appears inordinately bleak:
Nihilistic would be the word,
But that, against all evidence,
You celebrate what is, and God.
    This is supposed to be, however,

A congratulatory birthday letter,
And not an exercise in lit. crit.
I think perhaps it would be better
To turn on the nostalgia, and
Recall those evenings at the Ship
And Shovel, under Charing Cross,
And all those trains you used to miss
That ran from there to Sevenoaks;
Evenings with Higgins, Cliff, and Swift,
And Kavanagh glowering over
Scotch and bicarbonate of soda,
Those Celtic twilights of the past;
Or to recall the Dorset lanes
Haunted the less by Hardy's ghost
Than by the verse of William Barnes,
For you, most English of English;
Recall also, last but not least,
At Bemerton, the frugal church
George Herbert made a temple of:
For here I followed where you led.

   Time I signed off: I hope that I
May follow you to seventy!
I see you in your evening room
High above Parrett and the moors
Stretched to the trembling of a sky
Closed over Alfred's and Arthur's
Lands, the England of your eye
Made of the living and the dead,
And on the horizon a tower.
Happy returns.
                    As ever,
                         David.

## A Letter to John Heath-Stubbs

From Leeds, two dozen years ago
(Eheu fugaces! how they slide!)
You wrote to me in London: so
Here is an indolent delayed
Reply in kind, although the verse
Be hopalong compared with yours.
Thus, as your sixtieth year falls due
Out of the north I answer you
Who live in London, which has been
Bar some brief periods of exile
By Aire or Niger or the Nile,
Since you abandoned Oxford to
Shift with the shiftless in Soho,
Your only and your real home.
What you contemned in '53,
The politics of power, or
Of current schools of poetry
Seems very much the same today;
We have the mixture as before.
So, no comment! Change is in things,
And mutability in stones
Rather than in living beings
Whose ephemeral, stable patterns
Persist through generations;
And you persist. A sixth decade
Attained demands an accolade
– Few of our friends have won as far.
Talking of which, the news has come
As I write this, of Tom Blackburn,
That difficult and honest man,
Fortunate in his death beneath
The mountains he celebrated;
One whose verse had grown, like yours,
Out of a rhetoric, plain flowers
Rooted not in suffering
But in ordinary living.
He did what he could do, and wanted;
And if he died disappointed
Thinking no public note was taken

Of his verse, he was mistaken:
That is, he should have realized
How privately the good are prized.
As a poet he was not great,
Not original, but unique:
An involved, yet an objective
Analyst of failing love
Who proved his own predicament
With awkward and compassionate
Concision, not to display
The pain, but as medicament.
Yet I do not intend all this
As a lament for makaris;
Just to note that 'what it takes
In the living poetry stakes'
(The quote's from Kavanagh on Yeats)
Is what you and they have got,
Which is no less a matter of
Music, language, and image,
Than of personal courage
To be oneself and go on being,
To see oneself and go on seeing.

## To Norman Nicholson

As the crow flies we live quite near each other:
But the crow never flies across those mountains,
Those lakes and valleys, rivers and small streams.
Walls crawling up impossible slopes to skies
Blue as an eye or ponderous with rain.

All that we must avoid if we're to reach you:
We go by Workington, to catch the diesel
Edging along a bleak polluted coastline,
Dead foundries, slagheaps, and the yellow flower
Of smoke above Whitehaven; Windscale's dome.

And then there's Ravenglass, and the bird-haunted
Sand-dunes lagooning a derelict sea.
This, Norman, is your country and your home,
And where your verse lives rooted like a tree
To where it grows, feeding its leaves therefrom.

## Meetings

*To David Gascoyne*

Forty years ago we met
In a room in Beaumont Street.
Summer at Oxford: in St Giles,
By the Eagle and the Child
A candelabra is lit,
And chestnut petals drift.
I see you, tall and serious,
Angular, pacific, like
Some Anglo-Saxon image in
A psalter, a marginal saint.
I did not know who you were then,
But recognized the authentic,
So seldom to be met again:
What Kavanagh used to talk
About, 'the true Parnassian';
He knew, like you and Jack Yeats, that
The top of Parnassus is flat.

Other meetings, other years:
Venice in 1950, when
You stayed with Peggy Guggenheim,
But I would not meet millionaires;
Later in Paris, where you talked
As I'd not heard you talk before,
And at the dinner which you cooked,
I met Madame Picabia.
Few meetings in divided lives,
But those few were luminous
With the epiphanic commonplace:
Like your Woodbine packet seen
Inscribed 'mene, tekel, upharsin'.

Perhaps the best of all was when
Under Tennyson's Blackdown,
Together with your friend and mine
(Call him the tenant of Hearne Farm),
We paced along the sacred grove
– A ragged hedge and a few trees,
And only sacred because loved –
And watched the English evening fade
And darkness thickening the leaves,
Where no word needed to be said.

## Letter to Charles Causley

Dear Charles, I write this doggerel
From Portingale to wish you well.
Here summer burns, and I am in
What has become my other home
Far from the borders of the north
Where half my heart is laid in earth;
Out of this window I can see
A uniting, dividing sea
While the red ground I tread upon
Recalls the land where I was born,
Fanatic sunlit Africa
Just half a horizon away.
Are you, as I hope I am, well?
And are you really seventy
Which, Deus vult, I soon shall be?
Do you remember how we met
In the studio of Patrick Swift
At midnight, and in Camden Town,
When, after pub-close, we burst in
With bottles and bonhomie to
Welcome our stranger guest, the new
Sweet chanter from the Cyprus Well,
The ballad-maker from Cornwall?
Our paths have seldom crossed since then,
And more than thirty years have gone
By us, but with exchanges of
Poems, admiration, and love;
And times have changed, and friends been lost,
Till our real future's now the past,
The treasure we laid up for age.
As memory is the truest Muse,
You will, dear Charles, with your clear voice
And fingers by long practice more
Skilful, if possible, than before,
Singing to the Apollonic lyre
Continue to delight, and draw
Articulate from the Cyprus Well
A music pure and natural.

## For Donald Davie

The last and second time we met
You may remember: not for me,
But as the last time Eliot
Appeared in public – where was it?
Some prizegiving for poetry
Held in the stadium at Earl's Court –
An odd place for us both to be.
I think George MacBeth got the cheque.
But, as you do, I well remember
The old man bowed at last with age,
Old eagle, with a nose like one;
A courteous patrician,
His dying written in his face.
There we, amid car-salesmen's booths
That winter evening, '64,
One from the groves of Academe
The other from Bohemia's seacoast,
Crossed, not swords but paths, watching
The great man and the minor poets.

## For George Barker at Seventy

I see rain falling and the leaves
Yellowing over Eden, whose
Brown waters flood below the house
Where, thirty-five years on, I live.

So long it is since first we met,
And in another world, it seems,
Where, out of pocket, down at heels,
Night after night in Rathbone Place

The kings of Poland, and nowhere,
The out of kilter, or the good
For nothings, unfit misfits who'd
Been called to follow no career,

Would find themselves, and tell the truth.
Those great originals have gone,
They're either dead or on the wagon,
Shelved in a library, or the Tate:

But, like the Abbé, you survive.
The rain has stopped, and here's the sun
Bright gold, although it's westering:
The skies clear, and the leaves alive.

## In Memoriam David Archer

At the corner of a bar, lit by opaque windows,
*Times* and *New Statesman* still in their newsagent's folds, tucked
Under a withered arm shut like the wing of a bird,
Worried, inarticulate, dressed like a chief clerk,

David Archer that was, in the Wheatsheaf or Black Horse
– On Sundays at Notting Hill, the Old Swan or Windsor Castle,
A folder of plans toward some communal service
Clipped under the defeated arm as often as not.

A diffident but fanatic man; courteous;
Easily frightened; recovering courage, he'd look
Sidelong through spectacles, again like a bird, sharp and scared:
'I'm shaking like an aspirin tree. What'll you have?'

Neutral in a dark suit, holding a glass of Guinness,
That was his role and how he stood when the myths were made,
As necessary as a background and as modest,
Where they talked, struck light and took fire over his head.

Poured away and wasted like all valid sacrifice,
Libation of a subsistence. Died at Rowton House.
Impractical. Gone to immaterial reward
Along with Colquhoun and MacBryde, and Dylan Thomas.

## Franz Steiner Remembered

Franz, barely forty, an old man already:
His face had a scorched look. It is my fancy
Those burnings – books, then bodies, the nightmare
Of middle Europe, unimagined here –
Withered the skin of this lean survivor,
Always unlucky Franz, man without family
In exile from his language, living on.

Learned, caustic, an anthropologist who
Made Freud look foolish (that book on taboo,
The notes and MS lost at Paddington
With all the labour to be done again,
And done it was). Always unlucky Franz
Who'd cover up the mirrors in my room
– 'I do not want to see my face by chance' –
Whose reverence for his real vocation,
Weighing the syllables of words for verse
To draw upon the unknown to make known,
Would show up the dilletante I was.

Broken and not defeated, I see him
Comic in courage, at the telephone.
'But your voice sounds so strange – Franz, what is wrong?'
– 'I'm ringing from a call-box at the station.
My nose began to bleed, I'm upside down
And standing on my head' – the explanation.

## Winter Verses for Tambimuttu

What, in a letter to the dead,
Is better than to say what is?
Dear Tambi, as I write, the snow
Wheels slowly down, and will not stay;
And I am lost for words to say
This January afternoon.

Here is the view from my window:
Dark branches draw a skeleton
Tree against the fail of day,
And under, Eden's waters run
In stillness to the Irish sea.
They falter only at the ford

To etch a line of white across
Their moving motionless surface
As dark as the denuded boughs
That frame a glimmer in the west:
The sun that is about to die,
To burn tomorrow in the east.

I turn the leaves of memory
To see you, prince of Rathbone Place,
In blackout years, defying with
Magnanimous and careless spirit
A boring war, and holding court
In flyblown pubs for useless art;

You kept a spark alive, I think,
In that dead time, as dead as this
Midwinter landscape I look at,
Where, though the summer leaves be lost,
The living sap's in branch and root,
In ambush for a certain spring.

## West Penwith

*i.m. Kit Barker*

Cold lapis lazuli,
Rocks hung above a cove,
A harbour that the sea
Labours to remove,
And day by day succeeds.

All that was long ago:
Time changes, and times change;
Only an image
Alive within the mind
Of that scene, and of him,
Is now as it was then.

The lightshaft of Pendeen
Swings and illumines
Night in a seaward room
Where I no longer am.
Its light sweeps past a wall
Into the larger gloom,
Analogy of recall.

Noon Veor under a hill
And skyline of a moor:
Wind and the rain without,
Within a hearth as warm
As the heart of the host,
Where was a whole man
Happy and generous;
A grave comedian
Ear for the egregious,
And eye for the rum:
Gentleness where he was.

## For Paul Potts
*1911-1990*

'On mornings with no money but
The summer''s how I see you, Paul,
Holy liar lighting up
The true behind the factual:
An obsessed, imaginative
Compassion seeking out the real
And unapparent underdog
To champion Ezra and Campbell.

You romantic, realist
Wit, megasentimentalist;
Provider and connoisseur of
The grand theatrical gesture:
At and in poverty that forgives
For you, the failed and frustrate lives,
Die burning, saint and thief and child.

## An Encounter

The two of us there, talking animatedly.
He, trying to buy a way into our company?
The pub bore perhaps? Grey haired, a flushed ravaged
Complexion. Coat well cut; seen better days,
Like the Edwardian cut-glass and decor
And high pargeted ceiling of the bar.
'No, let me pay for it.' My companion's
Expression said, 'Don't let that chap horn in':
We were talking books, and people that we knew,
All strangers to the stranger. Even so,
Having myself been often on the fringe,
Not quite in nor quite out, though among friends,
I could not bring myself to give the brush-off.
Besides, he seemed to have the cash to waste:
Why say no to an offer to stand treat?
So let our new friend fork out for our beer,
And set myself to listen to the stranger.
Stranger? Unlike us, native to the place,
Newcastle-upon-Tyne. '. . . Seen better days?
Not many left; and money's nothing now.
Three months they give me, then I have to go.'

## An Appearance of Success

Some verses, written when he was alive,
A poster broadcast on the Underground;
My life (an actor plays him) televised;
Fame of a kind, if not recognition;
Pleasing enough but not enough to please
An unambitiousness at seventy-one,
Or pierce the unawareness of the dead:
This present I'd have loved to give to him
To make amends,
– My father – an appearance of success
In his deaf difficult son;
Something to recompense
As may have seemed to him
Rewardless and too long a sacrifice.

## Images for a Painter
*i.m. Patrick Swift 1927-1983*

I never imagined I
Should write your elegy.
I look out of the window
As you taught me to do.
All creation is grand.
Whatever is to hand
Deserves a line, praising
What is for being.

Thus at Westbourne Terrace
In long ago days
Brush in hand I'd see you
At your morning window
Transfer the thousand leaves
Of summer heavy trees
And delighting light
To another surface
Where they will not turn
With the turning season
But stay, and say
This is the mystery!
Or you would repeat
In pencil or in paint
The old stuffed pheasant too
That lived in your studio
Among the jars of turps
With a visiting ghost,
Charles Baudelaire's photo.
All the eye lights on
There for delighting.
Or put it this way,
A thing of beauty
Is joy perceived.
So you would give
Thanks for what is:
All art is praise.

Ah, those mornings
In many-hilled
Pombaline Lisbon!
The roads we travelled!
I do not mean
Only in Portugal –
Though now recalling
How, somewhere near
The river Guadiana
Going to Alcoutim,
We stopped the car
For, winding down
Round hills and bare,
Over no road came
The muleback riders
And blackshawled women
On foot, following
A coffin to nowhere:
Memento mori!

Or recollect
– Each one of us unique –
Your head suddenly
Thrown back, oblique
Eye over the laughter:
An aslant look
As if to say
Did the joke carry? The
Underlaid irony
Over the joke?

I see now
Out of my window
Mist rising from
A leaden Eden
Drifting slowly
Under trees barely
Leaved to the ford.
Gentle and aloud
The water breaks
As white as bread

Over the under road.
On the far bank
A field with trees
Each standing naked
On a fallen dress,
Brown and gold leaves.
I might relate
How swift my friend
Has gone, like these!
But I will not.
No cause for sadness,
You reader of Aquinas,
And clear Horace.
Whom the gods love, die
Young but not easily.

## Prospects

### I

Standing on Tara with Kavanagh
Wrapped in an old raincoat like
A scarecrow giant, and reminded
Of the other hill, Phaestos in Crete,
Of vastness and accurate light,
Though here the horizon is mist
And the wind is wet as Ireland;

It's somehow the same panorama,
Wide as the world is commonplace,
As ordinary as sacred;
The living, dead, romantic ghosts
Inhabiting the expressionless
Are genii loci here to lend a
Mirror to material nature.

I'd seen and thought the same upon
A high and Roman outpost set
Against the shoulder of Hardknott
Over the valley of the Esk,
With mountain following mountain
From wilderness to wilderness,
And tourist beercans in the grass.

Man is the measure, after all;
Distances are not curbed, but are
Fed and augmented by a wall,
Homestead or field; which remind us
The human being is central
To an indefinite universe
In which the earth is superstar.

It's twenty years or more since I
Stood on that royal windy hill;
Kavanagh cursing in the rain,
And not to be appeased until
We drove away in an old banger
In good time for the pub at Slane –
'No, it's your round,' – 'Black was the day

I met ye!' And the glasses fill.
Then back to Dublin and McDaid's,
A world that then seemed eternal,
But was ramshackle as our lives;
More fragile, even, as I find.
So many friends, so many graves.
I rake the ashes; last year's snows.


II

'Beth ware' – the doctor ends his tale –
'For no man woot whom God wol smyte.'
These were the very words I read
With no more thought than all was well;
Next day, three hundred miles away,
I stood by a hospital bed
In unbelief that he must die

His work half done: that Patrick Swift
With so much given, not yet old...
The spring was brilliant, not a cloud
In the March sky, and not a breath
Of wind disturbed the blue and gold
Day that lounged outside the glass
Pane where the world and living was.

Unlike and like as fingerprints
That never quite repeat a pattern,
We are, each one of us, in vision
And interpretation of what is,
Unique: a singular creation.
And yet with each a future dies
For more than for the dying one,

And even a past petrifies
When no new course or action can
Complete or modify what's been.
By that bed, in the banal sun,
There fell to me such thoughts as these.
In the renewal of the spring
I knew at heart no thing renews.

It took a year for him to die:
He had a year and more of grace,
Of sun and air; could even write
That all he looked upon was blessed;
And, looking at his canvases,
Convolute fig and almond groves
Set there by him, I know it was.

I said goodbye before he went.
That was the year when all was changed,
As changed as Algarve where he lived,
The once incommutable land
Bevilla'd, strung with golf courses,
With topless beaches, discothèques,
And fish and chips on every hand.

I'm in his tower studio
Where an Atlantic light comes in,
His easel set, dust gathering
Over the palette even now.
The figures of his forbears loom
From an unfinished landscape, half
Emergent, destined to remain

Shadows in a shadowy Wicklow:
The old ones, standing by their farm,
Must wait to be defined by him.
My friend, who cannot move his arm,
Or climb the tower stairs again,
Is breathing in a lower room,
And waiting for the light to go.

And as before, while the light fades,
We drink and speak; not as before:
For all we have to say is said,
Implicit in our being here.
And as we cannot look ahead,
Look back to find good fortune there:
The being that we both enjoyed

Which he can celebrate no more,
Or honour with reflecting hand.
Without his eyes I revisit
The cork oak forests of Monchique
That, stripped of bark above spring flowers,
Attend a far off Atlantic
Crawling to the Americas

Past the stone headland of Sagres.
Here is the café the forester
Sang like a lark in, while we ate
Partridges bedded in garlic
And drank Bemparece from Lagoa;
Here, Edwardian and embowered,
The gloomy purple-windowed spa

Dying in decorum and shade.
Or I look back at London years,
Talk of our scattered evenings –
MacDiarmid, Stevie, Kavanagh,
The Roberts, Barkers, and Behans,
Aleatory encounters
In Dean Street and in Fulham Road.

As for him, if he cannot speak,
As for me, if I cannot hear,
It's none the less a dialogue:
Between us the converse is clear.
For as his eye dulls or relumes
A legible response is there,
And I can read it at a glance.

## III

Not two months later he was dead:
And swift as waves break on the shore
Was followed by another death,
My mother's, in her hundredth year.
Too long a life for me to mourn
A love too great, like a gold chain
Too rich, too heavy to be borne.

And all I feel is, I am free.
If only I were not her son
Her sacrifice – but then I am;
Inhibited from fathoming
What I well know she did for me.
I move to the familiar room
Lit by a wintry August sun

Where she no longer is, although
The Magaliesberg mountain line
Still defines, framed in her window,
A built-up highveld's horizon;
Her absent presence manifest
Among inanimate bric-à-brac,
Her furniture, my photograph

Which I, first thing I do, take down –
That small boy in a floppy hat
She loved, whom I abominate –
And feel, as if I'd switched it off,
The life extinguish in the room.
It's the first change. You can't change back.
I knew, that moment, she had gone.

And gone with her, what histories
Obliterate, and characters
Legible only to her long
Remembering, finally consign
To dark and nowhere with her mind?
Snuffed out, what ghosts are at an end,
Gone with their last rememberer?

I am to take the ashes home.
Where are they? In a suitcase there.
And she will lie by Annan water,
By an ornate Victorian tomb
Beside her father and her mother,
And neighbour to the rufous sandstone
Provincial burgh she grew up in

But eluded ever after.
I look at her photograph, taken
Perhaps a week before she died,
Dressed elegantly for a wedding,
And, leaning over her, the bride:
Life, to the last, was for enjoying.
'I feel I should apologize

Like Charles II,' so she wrote
To me, 'to take so long in dying.'
And then there is a shopping list
Made out on what was her last morning:
'Be sure you bring me, when you come,
The brandy and face-powder, Helen.'
And here's the bottle, which I open.

When Jocomina Tsukulu
Rang her: 'The Madam is departing
From this life,' Helen found her dead,
Her eyes closed by the African.
'I wouldn't have known what to do.
These Africans, of course they know
All about death,' as Helen said:

Thus the last service was performed
By the true unacknowledged friend
Part loved, part hated, part abused,
With whom she quarrelled to the end,
Without whom she could not have lived,
And by whom was understood,
But whom she did not understand.

Which goes for me, and all of us.
I'll not see Africa again
I think. So before going home
I take the highroad for a last
Look at the land where I was born:
And, driving north by Pilgrim's Rest
– A tin-walled gold prospector's town

Nudged in a kloof behind the Berg's
Blind granite stonecliffs from whose verge
You spy, two thousand feet below,
The lowveld endless as a sea
Stretch flatly till it meets the sky
Or the sky meets it – finally
I end up in the Game Reserve

Where beasts are cared for better than
My fellow-townsmen, whose bare plots
And mud shacks make a desert of
The nowhere they are banished in.
But I've been lucky with my skin;
Am able therefore to admire
The thousands of impala,

Of zebra, sable, wildebeeste;
The ambling mastheads of giraffe,
And blunt, topheavy elephant
Browsing on treetops black with drought;
Or wingbeat of a hovering
Kingfisher with downbent beak
Intent above a shallow river.

Fenced in by homo sapiens,
The multiplicity of creation
Surviving in this museum Eden
And daily gaped at from machines,
Is counter to the actual
And outside world, the one we've made
A nightmare of, to service greed.

But should we blame intelligence?
We do not know what is to be
Any more than these innocent
And unpitying beasts of prey,
Or fleet birds and horned ruminants
That live for the indifferent day
And neither fear nor hope tomorrow's.


IV


Here is as far as I shall go –
A bluff above Olifants River
Looking toward the Lebombo
Mountains where the sun rises over
Bushveld as level as a table,
As vatic a panorama
As Phaestos or the hill of Tara:

Thus I am back where I began.
Perched on a cliff, the rondavel
I sleep in overlooks the sand
Bed of the Olifants below
That nourishes a foliage
Which is the brown land's only green,
And brings the kudu here to graze.

An historyless primeval
Wilderness with no memories,
With not a myth or ghost or fable,
Whose retrospects are yet to come.
I watch the sun, a bloody eyeball,
Climb up and clear the mists of morning
That blear a prospect of nothing,

Africa, tabula rasa!
Resolved upon no resolution
I pack my bag, and throw away
Souvenirs of too short a stay –
Let them take the next comer in!
And turn to trace the road I came
From illusion to illusion.

*Patrick Kavanagh, 1909-1967*
*Patrick Swift, 1927-1983*
*Jean Murray Wright, 1881-1983*

## A Charm

To send you sleep I send you images.

A full moon building a pacific ocean
Your boat floats in the middle of; a world
Of black air and flat water; blind as silence.

A shallow valley below bowing mountains,
A force so far off you don't see it move,
Hung between mountains berried rowans bower.

A Sunday; jacarandas line the square;
Aloes, azulejos, a white church tower;
A nun in sunlight, patient as prayer.

To send you sleep I blend you images.

## An Elegy
*Phillipa Reid 1927-1985*

These verses you will never read,
For you, beloved friend, are dead.
Under a mountain, by a lake,
Your ashes for my ashes wait.
I have been silent for too long,
Dumbstruck by that oblivion
I am to share and never know.
Beloved, it is high summer now,
Your roses blowing, each petal
Consummate and ephemeral,
Emblems of joy you and I,
Two persons in the one body,
So often granted to each other.

But I look back to that October
And ordinary autumn morning,
The air and banal sunlight glowing;
You sit upon a kitchen chair
Abstracted. Then you are not there.
An absence slowly apparent:
The body moves, and you aren't in it.

\*

As ephemeral as a rose
The art, the vocation that chose
Her from the ruck, to illumine
What we are, can be, or have been:
A voice, a body on a stage
To define, interpret, appraise
With passion correlative
To the perception of what is;
Art living in a living now
With nothing but recall to show
At curtain fall, performance over,
The solidity of a sculpture
For ever valid, even though
Made for the moment, made for now,

51

Conterminous as that rose,
And fading as a moment fades.

A last chat in the hospital,
A brave face and frightened eye:
It breaks my spirit to recall
That goodbye, casual and final.
Then nine days' coma, to awake
Unable to so much as speak,
But hearing, understanding all.
The long blind corridors I trod,
And ghastly pavements glinting rain,
That fardel of a hopeless hope –
'Technically successful, the op.,
But –.' Never to come back again.

'Love at first sight' – no, never that;
But for me, when our glances met
That Sunday in Lamb's Conduit Street,
Half-guessing at what lay ahead,
I recognized the other half
Of what I'd be, not what I was,
Brought by a destiny or good luck.

Today, the 24 July,
Her birthday. I recall the first
We shared – it was her twenty-fourth –
The packet, Dieppe-Newhaven,
Butting across a windy Manche
With us on board her, en retour
From castle-building days in Spain
Where she had given her promise
To waste it for the sake of mine:
Unselfseeking, too generous
To win that token, token fame.
All I could give was happiness,
A happiness she did not want,
Preferring the acknowledgement
Of anon, an audience.

What she gave me was all she had,
Was it then nothing, that I gave?
You get no answer from the dead,
You cannot parley with a grave.

And all that's left is memory.
I cannot visualize her face.
Here is her image on a leaf
Of paper, freeze-dried from the life,
A shadow; and she is a shade.

And there are letters; shadows too
Of an accord. Two minds, but one
Enjoyment of reality:
A making light of common day,
Oblique, ironic perception
Of aboriginal comedy.

So many gifts, except for one
Which in the end annulled them all:
Virtuosity; natural skill;
A naked body's perfection;
Intelligence, that illumines
And illustrates the beautiful;
Courtesy, courage, compassion,
All these, bar the one gift not given,
Ever unlucky, of good fortune.

Half of me, as I know, is gone,
And more than half; see what a swathe
The winter cut! So few are left
Of those who made me what I am.
It is another ambience
I now live in, although the same
River my window under dawdles,
The same thrush props about the lawn
Marauding; the same chaffinch startles.
I know it is not her I mourn,
It is myself, a lost I am.

## Five Elegies

*i.m. Phillipa Reid*

### After Cino da Pistoia
*c.1270-1337*

i

In fields I look for each white flower
Remembering what makes me sigh.

It's her white blouse that I remember
When the sharp arrow of Venus' archer
Lodged in my heart. When a light air
Lifts a white petal, I remember
The sweeter white of her eye
And my desire is for ever.


ii

I was upon the high and happy mountain
I loved, and stumbled on that headstone
Where honesty laid a forehead down,
And which shut off all virtues' fountain
That day when through death's bitter pass
Was thrust the woman of my heart –
Alas that beauty, alas that charm.

There it was I made this prayer
To love: Let death take me here,
Because my love lies here,
But when love did not hear
I left, still calling upon her,
And so passed
A voice of sorrow
The mountain over.

## A Question

Does love, dear love, survive a grave?
Forever absent while I live
And constant in a silence
No news will ever break,
There by the margin of a lake
Rests a boxed oblivion
I would speak to, that will not speak.

And sadder is that northern lake,
Now sadder for me than Avernus'
Bare water, denuded of great
Bowering woods, Virgilian leaves,
Where, under what seemed English skies
Cold, clouded, and subfusc,
We picnicked, what time Cerberus
(Or so we called the dog, remember?)
Strolled up to us, and fed by her
As in the fable fell asleep.

I raised a question, got no answer,
Yet was answered after all
In that moment of recall,
My love living while I live.
Over time and grief prevail
Recollections: all she is.

## From a Southern Window

I do not purpose to awake
A living sorrow that's asleep:
Time is anaesthetic, sure
To do the job. A clear November
Light wasting through a southern window
Two years, a thousand miles away
From that other window looking
Over a valley of the Tyne,
Recalls a light too well remembered:

The same light breaking through its pane,
Illumining a long dying,
A losing hope, an end of loving.

An Aegean, Hebridean
Light, the light of Italy,
Through the hospital window shone
All day all that St Martin's summer;
The last thing that we saw together
To wonder at, was its dead sun
Upon spread embers of the west
With eastern darkness coming up:
We, in our admiration
– I did not, she could not, speak –
Made a last communication.

*Alfanzina, 1987*

## Those Walks We Took

Those walks we took I shall not take
Again. The meadows sloping to
A wooded, sunken, mud-brown beck
Where, brilliant, a kingfisher flew
A flash beneath a wooden bridge,
I shall not see: but recollect,
And so preserve a living Now
In which my loss may figure like
The autumnal and failing light
That washed the fields with dying gold.

Often we walked along that beck
And crossed its rotting bridge to find
The white farmhouse below the falls
Sometimes Niagara, sometimes
A straggle like a gap-toothed comb:
And where its water dug a pool
Were Christmas geese, and water-fowl,
Making a picture for the mind
To keep – no, not for ever, but
As long as one of us had breath.

*Et in Arcadia*

i

Living is here
And now. I
Look forward, see
Today tomorrow
A yesterday
Of what was I
When we were.


ii

All is recalling: how
Our vision of what's gone
Changes with each new Now
As we change with what's done
And our perspectives change.
Life, they say, must go on
To alter all, to alter
In recollection
That shadow of her shadow,
All of her that I am.


iii

The sun on a polluted river,
May morning by a flowing Thames,
A lace of trees, their leaves beginning,
And we two strangers holding hands
Beside a theatre yet a-building,
By broken bricks and iron bones
Of weathered bomb-sites weeding over
In sunlight that's presaging summer,
A summer that has come, and gone.

iv

Et in Arcadia
Ego. As evening
Leads her shadow on
And, diamond, a star
Increases with the wane
Of light to promise a
Different beginning,
I am to thank whatever for
The fortune of day.


v

I am changing: she does not.
How can I change and she not change?
Those words, Till death do us part,
Too late I understand.
I see things in a different dark,
All things that nothing can explain.

## After Charles d'Orléans

The year has thrown away its gear
Of wind and snow, of frost and rain,
And put on a regalia
Of sunlight, brilliant and clear.
   No creature of the earth or air
But sings or shouts in its own tongue:
The year has thrown away its gear
Of wind and snow, of frost and rain.
   Spring and rivulet and river
Wear like a joyous livery
Silver drops and jewelry,
There's a new dress for everything.
The year has thrown away its gear.

## The Pair

AFTER HUGO VON HOFMANNSTHAL

She bore the beaker in her hand
– Her profile rounded as its rim –
Her footsteps were so light and firm
No drop from it slopped to the ground.

As light and steady was his hand;
He rode a young and restive horse,
And with a careless casual grace
Brought it, trembling, to a stand.

And yet, when from the lady's hand
He was to take the buoyant cup,
It proved too heavy for the pair:
They trembled, both of them, so much
That neither found the other's hand;
The red wine spurted to the earth.

## Neue Liebe

AFTER HEINRICH HEINE

In moonlight in the forest I saw the elves go riding
Their horns I heard sounding, the jingling of their bells,
Their ponies white and antlered flying by
Like wild swans, strung against the sky;
Their queen, she bends her head to me and smiles.
Now does it mean a new love, or that I am to die?

## Nobody

AFTER JUAN RAMOS JIMENEZ

'It was nobody – water.' 'Nobody?
Is water nobody?' 'Nobody –
A flower.' 'Is there nobody?
But is a flower nobody?'

'Nobody but the wind.' 'Nobody?
Is the wind nobody?'
'Nobody – delusion.' 'There is nobody?
And is delusion nobody?'

## Autopsicographia

*O poeta e um fingador*

The poet is counterfeiter,
Counterfeits so well
He counterfeits the sorrow
That for him is real.

And those who read his poem
Feel not what he felt,
They feel its single sorrow,
And not his double hurt.

So round and round its railway,
Reason to divert,
Runs the wound-up toy
That people call the heart.

## Song
AFTER FERNANDO PESSOA

*Silfos ou gnomos tocam? . . .*

Music of faun or dryad? . . .
Rustle of pinewoods
Shadows, zephyrs,
A harmony.

Floats undulant
Like a winding road
Or, among trees,
One who, appearing,
Disappears.

Far uncertain echo
Of what I'll never
Have . . .
Half heard, bringing
Tears – why I'm weeping
I do not know.

So soft a harmony,
Do I hear it, or
Only the melancholy
Of twilights, pinewoods,
And I.

But ceases, as a breeze
Forgets its breath.
Now is no music,
Rustle of pinewoods.

## Between Sleep and Dream
AFTER FERNANDO PESSOA

*Entre o sono e o sonho*

Between sleep and dream,
The I am and what I am,
And who I think I am,
A river
Runs for ever.

Ran between other
Far and varying
Banks, this river,
In the divers
Voyagings
Of any river.

It arrived
Where I live,
The house that's I
Today. Runs by
If I muse on
Myself. – Awaken
And it has gone.

He whom it seems
To me I am,
And he who dies
In that which binds
Me to I am –
Sleeps where that river
Runs for ever.

## Dom João Primeiro
AFTER FERNANDO PESSOA

*O homem e a hora são um só*

Man and hour are as one
When God acts, to shape
History; the rest
Is flesh and bone,
Dust earth awaits.

Unawares master
Of the Temple
That became Portugal;
Her glory's harvester
Whose example
Served to defend her.

Your name, elect of fame,
At our hearts' altar
Shifts – an eternal flame –
The eternal shadow.

## Mar Portugues
AFTER FERNANDO PESSOA

*Ó mar salgado, quanto do teu sal*

Salt is the sea and above all
Salt with the tears of Portugal.
With how many mothers' tears
And how many useless prayers,
Tears of brides who sleep alone,
That the sea should be our own.

Worth the pain? But what is not
If the soul be great enough?
Who sails beyond the ocean's rim
At Bojador, sails beyond pain.
Deep and perilous the sea
God made for mirroring the sky.

## Da mais alta janela da minha casa
AFTER FERNANDO PESSOA

From my highest window
With a white handkerchief I wave
Goodbye to my poems departing.
And I'm neither glad nor sorry.
It's what happens to poems.
I made them and so I must show them
Because I have to:
A flower can't hide its colour,
Nor a river its flowing,
Nor a tree its fruit.

There they go, already distant, as if they'd been driven off in a taxi,
And I feel, despite myself,
Grief like a bodily pain.

Who can tell who'll read them?
Into whose hands will they fall?

Flower: it is my fate to be picked for eyes to see.
Tree: they took my fruit for mouths to eat.
River: it is my fate to flow and not contain.
I acquiesce, and almost feel happy
As almost happy as when fed up with feeling sad.

Go, go from me!
The tree dies and spreads over Nature.
The flower fades and its pollen is eternal.
The river flows to the sea and its water remains always its own.

Like the universe, I go and I stay.

## The Tobacconist's
AFTER FERNANDO PESSOA (ALVARO DE CAMPOS)

Am nothing.
Will never be anything but nothing.
Can't even want to be nothing.
On the other hand there are in me all the dreams of the world.

Windows of my room,
My room, myself one of the world's millions nobody knows anything about
(And if they did, what would they know?),
You look out upon the enigma of a street which people are continually
    crossing,
A street inaccessible to thought,
Real, impossibly real, actual, beyond understanding actual,
With enigma under the stones and living beings,
With death to dampen the walls and whiten the hair,
With Fate driving a cartload of all along the road of nullity.

Just now I'm done for, as if I knew the truth.
Just now my head's clear, as if I were about to die,
And had no more to do with things
Than leavetaking, this house and this side of the street
Turning into a line of railway carriages, the signal for their departure
Whistled from inside my head,
A jolting of nerves, and grating of bones, as it moves off.

Just now I'm confused, as if I'd thought and found out and forgotten.
Just now I'm split between the allegiance I owe
To the tobacconist's on the other side of the street, as something externally
    real,
And to the feeling that everything is a dream, as something inwardly
    true.

I've failed at everything.
As I had no aims, it was probably nullity.
That apprenticeship I was given –
I dropped out of it through the back window of the house.
I went out into the country with great expectations.
But there I only came across grass and trees,
And when there were people they were all the same as one another.

69

I turn from the window, sit down in a chair. What have I to think about?

Be a genius? At this moment
A hundred thousand brains are dreaming, like me, they are geniuses,
And – who knows? History will probably take no note, not one,
Nor will anything but dung be left of so many future conquests.
No, no, I don't believe in myself.
All the madhouses are full of lunatics full of certainties!
I who am certain of nothing, am I the more or less certain?
No, not even of myself.
In how many garrets and non-garrets of the world
Are there not, at this very moment, self-professed geniuses dreaming?
How many high aspirations, pure and noble aspirations,
– Yes, genuinely noble and pure –
Will never be heard of nor see the actual light of day?
The world is for those who were born to conquer
And not for those who imagine they can conquer it, even if that makes
    sense.
I've imagined more than Napoleon ever achieved.
I've hugged to a hypothetical breast more humanity than Christ,
I've conceived, in private, philosophies that no Kant ever wrote.
But I am, and will probably always be, the man in the garret,
Even if I don't live there;
I'll always be *the one not born for it*;
I'll always be *the one who had potentialities*;
I'll always be the one who waited for them to open the door at the foot
    of a wall without a door,
And sang the song of the Infinite in a henhouse,
And heard the voice of God in a lidded well.
Believe in myself? No, not in anything.
Pour over my burning head, Nature,
Your sun, your rain, your wind that lifts my hair.
And the rest that may come if it will, or must come, or not come.
Sick hearts enslaved by the stars,
We've conquered the entire globe before getting out of bed;
But woke up and all is fog,
Got up and all's alien,
Went out of the house and it's the whole earth,
Plus the solar system, the Milky Way, and the Infinite.

70

(Little girl, eat up your chocolates!
Eat your chocolates!
The only metaphysics in the world are chocolates, see?
All the religions teach no more than the confectioner.
Eat up, you filthy little girl, eat up!
Would I could eat chocolates with the same factuality!
But I think and, having unwrapped the silver paper – i.e. tinfoil –
Drop it all on the ground, just as I do with life.)


But at least there remains, from the exacerbation of what will never be,
The swift cursive of these verses,
A broken portal to the impossible.
But at least I devote myself to a dry-eyed disdain
Noble, at least, in the grand gesture of casting
The soiled clothes that are me (no list) into the course of things,
To stay at home without a shirt.


(You who console, who do not exist, and therefore console,
Whether a Greek goddess, conceived as a statue that may come alive,
Or Roman Lady, inconceivably noble and malign,
Or troubadour princess, none more lovely and radiant,
Or eighteenth-century marchioness, remote and décolletéed,
Or cocotte, celebrated in our fathers' day,
Or merely something modern – I really can't think what –
All this – whatever it is – you must be, and if it can inspire, inspire!
My heart is an emptied garbage-can.
Those who invoke spirits, invoke spirits; likewise I invoke
Myself, and find nothing.
I go to the window and see the street with perfect clarity.
I see the shops, the pavements, cars passing,
I see live garmented beings walk by,
I see the dogs (they too are alive)
And all this weighs upon me like a sentence of banishment
And it's all alien, like all things.)


I have lived, learned, loved, even believed,
And now there's not a beggar I don't envy because he isn't me.
I look at their rags and ulcers and lies
And think, perhaps you've never lived, nor learned, nor believed,

(Because it's possible to make all this real without doing any of all that);
Perhaps you have hardly existed, like a lizard when its tail's cut off
And it's a tail wriggling away from its lizard.

I turned myself into I don't know what,
And what I could make of myself I didn't make.
The cloak I put on was the wrong one.
They knew me at once for someone I wasn't, and I didn't deny it and was
    lost.
When I tried to pull off the mask
It stuck to my face.
When I got it off and saw myself in the glass
I had grown old.
I was drunk, I didn't know how to put on the cloak I hadn't taken off.
I threw away the mask and went to sleep in the cloakroom
Like a dog the management tolerates
Because it isn't a nuisance
And I'm about to write this story to prove I am sublime.
Musical essence of my useless verses,
I wish I could find in you something that I had made
And not stay always facing the tobacconist's opposite,
Treading underfoot the consciousness of being alive
Like a carpet a drunk trips over
Or a doormat stolen by gypsies, worth nothing.

But the owner of the tobacconist's has come to the door and stands in
    the doorway.
I look at him with unease, as if I'd a kink in the neck,
With the unease of a soul with blurred vision.
He'll die, and I'll die.
He'll abandon his signboard, and I my verses.
One day the signboard will also perish, and the verses too.
In time the street where the signboard was will perish,
And the language in which the verses were written.
After that the spinning globe where all this happened will perish.
On other planets in other systems something like people
Will go on making things like poetry and living under things like sign-
    boards,

Always one thing opposite another,
Always one thing as useless as another,
Always the impossible as inept as the actual,
Always the enigma of profundities, as certain as the sleep of the surface
     enigma,
Always one thing or another, or neither one thing or another.

But a man has gone into the tobacconist's – to buy tobacco? –
And the believable actuality suddenly descends upon me.
I half-rise, energetic, convinced, human,
And determine to write these verses in which I say the opposite.

I light a cigarette while I contemplate writing them
And taste in the cigarette a liberation from all ideas.
I follow the smoke as if it were an appropriate guide,
And savour, for one sensitive and cogent moment,
Freedom from all speculations,
And the consciousness that metaphysics is a consequence of feeling
     poorly.
Then I lean back in my chair
And go on smoking.
While Fate permits I shall go on smoking.
(Were I to marry the daughter of my washerwoman
Perhaps I'd be happy.)
At this I heave myself up from the chair. I go to the window.

The man has come out of the tobacconist's (putting change in his trousers
     pocket?)
Oh, I recognize him: it's Esteve, a man without metaphysics.
(The tobacconist has come to the door.)
As if by divine instinct, Esteve turns round and sees me,
He waves a greeting, I shout back *Hullo Esteve!* and the universe
Reassembles itself without an ideal or a hope, and the tobacconist smiles.

## Six Poems of Alberto Caeiro
AFTER FERNANDO PESSOA

*Não me importo com as rimas*

Not to bother with rhymes. Rarely
Are two trees alike, side by side.
As flowers have colour
I think and write, but say
What I have to say less perfectly
Because I lack the divine
Naturalness of being wholly
What I am.

What I see moves me.
I am moved, as water runs
When the ground inclines,
And my verses are as natural as the breathing of the wind.


*Olá, guadador de rebanhos*

'Ho there, herdsman! You there
On the road's verge! What does it say,
The wind, as it blows by?'

'That it is wind, that it blows by
As before it has blown by,
And will again blow by.
But to you, what does it say?'

'Many other things, many more,
To me it has much to say:
Memories, nostalgia,
And things that never were.'

'Never did you hear the wind.
The wind says wind only.
What you heard was a lie,
And in yourself is the lie.'

*Dizes-me: tu és mais alguma coisa*

You're telling me that you're something better
Than a plant or a stone.
You're telling me that you feel, think, and know
That you think and feel.
Then do stones write verses?
Do plants have ideas then?

Right you are, there's a difference.
But it's not the one you think it is;
For being sentient doesn't mean I've got to have theories about things,
It only means I've got to be aware.

Am I better than a plant or stone? Don't know.
Am different. Don't know if that's better or worse.

Better to have awareness than the hues of a flower?
Perhaps; or perhaps not.
All I know is, it's different.
No-one can prove it's anything other than different.

I know that a stone is real, and that a plant exists.
This I know because they are.
This I know because my senses declare it.
I know also that I am real.
This I know because my senses declare it,
Though with less acuity than when they show me a plant or a stone.
More than this I do not know.

Right you are: I make verses, and stones do not;
Right you are: I have ideas, and plants haven't.
But stones aren't poets; they're stones;
Plants are plants, not philosophers.

I might as soon say I'm superior to them
As that I'm their inferior.
But I don't. I say of a stone, 'Here's a stone',
I say of a plant, 'Here's a plant',
I say of myself, 'Here I am',
And say nothing more. What more to say?

75

*Antes o vôo da ave...*

Rather the flight of a bird that flies past leaving no trace,
Than the print of an animal that leaves remembrance on the ground.
The bird goes by and is forgotten, which is as it should be.
The animal, although no longer here and so of no importance,
Manifests its having been; this too is of no importance whatever.

Remembering is to be false to Nature
For the Nature of yesterday is not Nature.
That which was is nothing: to remember is not to see.
Go, bird, go, and teach me how to go!


*A espantosa realidade das coisas*

The stupendous actuality of things:
This is what I discover each day.
Each thing is what it is,
And it's not easy to explain how that elates,
How, for me, it's enough.

It is enough to exist to be perfect.

I've written poems enough.
I shall write plenty more, naturally.
Each poem says it,
And all my poems are different,
Because each thing that is has a way of saying it.

Sometimes I look at a stone.
I don't wonder if it is sentient,
I don't go through the business of calling it my sister,
But I like it because it is a stone,
I like it because it is not sentient,
I like it because it bears no relation to myself.

At other times I hear the wind blow,
And it seems to me that it is worth the pain of being born only to hear
    the wind blow.

I don't know what people will think when they read this;
But it seems to me that it has to be good because the thought came to
    me unhindered
Without the notion that other people would be attending;
Because the thought came to me without my thinking,
Because I say it as the words that came to me say it.

There was a time when they called me a realist,
Which astonished me, because I never supposed
That anybody could call me anything.
I'm not even a poet. All I do is see.
If what I write has value, the merit is not mine:
The merit is there, in my verses.
All of this is wholly independent of my own volition.


*Ha metafisica bastante...*

Metaphysics enough in not thinking of anything.
What's my idea of the world?
Who knows?
But if I fell ill, I'd think of it.

What's my notion of things?
My ideas concerning cause and effect?
My ruminations on God and the soul and the entire creation?
I don't know. For me, thinking about such things is like shutting the eyes
And not thinking – like drawing the curtains
Of my window (supposing it had any curtains).

The mystery of things? What mystery?
There's only one mystery: folk thinking about mystery.
If you stand in the sun and shut your eyes
You begin to lose sight of the sun
And to think of the heat.
But open your eyes and see the sun,
Then you can't think of anything,
For the light of the sun is more valid than the thought
Of any philosopher, of any poet.
The light of the sun does not know what it does,
Therefore does not err: is universal and good.

Metaphysics? What metaphysics in those trees over there?
Those of greenery and shade, of the spreading of their boughs,
Of bearing their fruit in season: which does not make us think,
Not us, who do not spare them a thought.
But what better metaphysics than theirs – not
To know what they live for,
Not to know that they do not know?

*The inner constitution of matter*
*The inner meaning of the universe –*
All this is fallacy, so much hot air.
It beats me that anyone can think of such things.
It's like thinking of means and ends
In the first glimmer of dawn, when over there by the trees
A lustre of faint gold confounds the dark.

Mulling over the inner meaning of matter
Is a bit much, like mulling over well-being,
Or taking a glass to spring water.
There's only one inner meaning of matter:
There's no inner meaning whatever.

Nor do I believe in God – I've never seen him.
Did he want me to believe
No doubt he'd come and speak,
Come in through my door
And say to me, *Here I am!*

(This perhaps sounds absurd to the ears
Of those who, because they don't know how to observe,
Don't understand those who talk of things
In the way that looking at them teaches.)

But if God is the flowers and trees
The mountains, the sun, and the light of the moon,
Well then, I believe in him,
Well then, at all times I believe in him,
And my whole life is a prayer and a festival,
A communion through my eyes and ears.

But if God is the flowers and trees
The mountains, the sun, and the light of the moon,
Why do I call him God?
I call him flowers and trees and mountains, the sun, and the light of the
    moon,
Because he has made himself, that I might see him,
Sun and the light of the moon, flowers and trees and mountains,
He manifests himself as trees and mountains,
As moonlight, as sun, and flowers,
Which means that he wants me to know him
As trees, mountains, flowers, moonlight and sun.

And that's why I obey,
(What more do I know of God than God himself?)
I obey by living instinctively
Like one who opens his eyes and sees,
And call him moonlight and sun and flowers and trees and mountains,
And love him without thinking,
And think of him by seeing and hearing:
At all times I am with him.